ATTENTION SEEKER

Attention Seeker

A BOOK OF POETRY

Harry Ward

The Hobservatory

About the author

I was born in 1986
in Kingston Upon Thames, England
and 37 years later I wrote this book.

About the book

This book is a collection of my poems
from the years up to and including 2023.
They are all arranged in a very specific order,
but I'm not going to tell you what it is.

I would not have made any of these poems public
had it not been for a brief flirtation with a girl I
met on holiday. She told me my poems were cool.
I'll let you be the judge.

H.W.

"It's just a ride..."

- Bill Hicks

A Common Misconception

Sweeping landscapes of past and future
You're overwhelmed by the beauty
But it'll pass
You're just new here

West of Country

As the course gale-force town is coloured by grey
Residents flee to their homes, as night takes the day
Little vampires gather in the twilight to play
Much to the citizen's ignorant dismay

Time has forgotten this broken mould
With no change in sight before young become old
Visionary directions
Scary reflections

This place
This town
This face
This frown

Is it really so bad, or is everything fine?
It must just be this head of mine

Where the Heart Is

Games that are played on the beach and parade
Belong not just to us but the people before
As they did, we reside here, with tradition and lore
Generations of families
Lovers
Memories of War

Our town
Our history
Our affection
No mystery

We have loved this place
Forever we have loved this place
Smiles on our faces
No matter our creeds or races

For this is our home
Where we live
Where we die
Together
And alone
This is our home

Broaden Your Horizons

Sit quietly and wait
Do a drawing
Tousle your hair
Look over there
I can't afford this patience
Wait enough to crush bone
So, what am I to do?
Sit quietly and wait
Alone

YVGTYRWHLLFHDFY

Everyone seems to know what they are doing
But how have they come to their conclusions
I'm sat here with all my confusions
Still trying to figure out what I want to be when I grow up
Sometimes I wonder
Whether I'm actually here...

Attention Seeker

Please be quiet, everyone can hear you
I get it, you got to let it out
You "need" to
But if you could limit your angst
I'd appreciate it
Thanks

You Were Warned

Yeah, yeah, I gave you the wrong impression
Well maybe consider this a lesson
You can't blame someone else for your own mistake
How much responsibility are you going to take?
None. Exactly. That is just so you
Cross off be a hypocrite from your list of 'things to do'
Now seriously, grow up. Think about this
You're getting emotional, don't create a crisis
You clearly misunderstood me and now you've learned
That when you play with fire you might get burned
Maybe in the future you'll take a little more care
Oh, and talk back to me again
Go on, it's a DARE

Qué

How can you take such advantage of me?
It is a disorder of your personality

How can I take it when you are so mean?
Because I have little to no self esteem

What do we do while this life passes by?
Keep saying, "I love you". Keep telling a lie

What does one do when the broke heart stops beating?
Remember the good times, and how they were fleeting

A Slightly Dishonest Flirtation With the Past

You filled my heart
Until it burst
The day we met
I've all but cursed
I wouldn't be
Who I am now
If you had not
Fucked me up somehow

You consumed my unconditional love
An insatiable appetite, me wasn't enough

A predator inside
My troubled psyche
Convinced my self esteem
No one else liked me
Some hateful spectre
A ghost in the past
I'm so glad that you're gone
And 'we' didn't last

A Slightly Dishonest Flirtation With the Past (cont.)

Seek sustenance now
In the pain of others
As my feelings for you
I've completely smothered
The love, the care
The spite, the hate
Time to stop saying sorry
It's way, way too late

...now spit

Practicing your emotional dentistry

I should have listened

When you said,

  "This is going to hurt you

    A lot more

    Than it does me"

OH MY GOD GET OVER IT

You know, I can understand why people go
Back to an abusive partner
Company
Being alone is harder

Loneliness hurts
The pain the heart exerts
It feels like internal bleeding
It feels like eternal needing
Time slows down then starts to repeat
While no one seems aware of your solitary retreat
You step back from life so the loneliness makes sense
Because you had your chance at happiness

Had – past tense

I'm sure alone one can manifest one's own destiny
I'd just prefer to do it with somebody next to me

Routine

Happier now, for the time being
But it won't last

It feels like it will at the moment
But it won't last

Combative feelings will keep me in bed
I'll infer stranger's opinions of me
No one will see me for days
My personal hygiene will suffer
But it won't last

Obsessive compulsion will take over
My bedroom will be spotless
Early morning runs, no smoking, no alcohol
I'll banish sugar and dairy from my diet
But it won't last

Routine (cont.)

There will be a road trip to nowhere and back
Without even leaving the car
Shopping will consist of 7g of one thing
And 700ml of something else
Workdays become mainly absent excuses
Crumbs and creatures will share my bed
But it won't last

My eyes will open before the alarm, fresh and clear
Rather than drive, I'll walk into town
Smiling at every passer-by
I'll have coffee al fresco and watch everyone
Doing their daily whatevers
Feeling like a strong individual
Basking in my potential
But it won't last

Tell Me, Please

Why have things that can't be shared

Why be brave when you are scared

Why be present when now has passed

Why fall in love when it won't last

Why grow flowers when they will die

Why be honest when you can lie

Why collect thoughts when memories fade

Why ask when your mind is made

Why have dreams while you're awake

Why keep giving when you can take

Tell Me, Please (cont.)

Why rush life when there is time

Why shed tears when everything's fine

Why believe when there is truth

Why waste time while in your youth

Why have things that you can't share

Why live life when you don't care

What is the Point

a positive nihilist
real life is realest

god is not teaching us
all life is meaningless

Commitments

Don't be sad
Wake up feeling
It's not so bad
Floor's now ceiling
Spring was loaded
Fall down
Poor show, kid
Ball gown
Honest make-up
Lying still
Triggered shake up
Crushes will
Skin's peeling
Every way
Wake up feeling
Every day

Applied Logic

Nobody tells a joke
As well as a stranger

Nobody disappoints you
As much as a family member

In this world of fear
There is no imminent danger

Except for living without experience
And in old age
Having nothing to remember

RUOK

Write words
Wrong time
Half hearted
Skipping beats
Run out of racy things...
Touché

Right words
Questioned talent
Left marks
Miss company
Missed a chance
Bad language
No sé

SUPERPOSITION

THE WINDOW BECAME A SCREEN DISPLAYING
A FANTASY I NEVER HAD. AN ODD FEELING
OF DETACHMENT FROM A WORLD I CREATED.
GRADUALLY, AS I TRAVELLED THROUGH TIME
I FOUND MYSELF IN SUPERPOSITION. MY
EXISTENCE DEFINED BY OTHERS OBSERVATION
OF MY BEING. YOU CAN'T SEE ME WHEN YOU'RE
NOT THERE WHILE AT THE SAME TIME I'M
EVERYWHERE. BETWEEN OTHER PEOPLE'S
REALITIES I'M NOT SEEING. IT'S PARALYSING,
THAT FEELING. WAS I EVEN PRESENT? WAS I
PAST? I COULDN'T TELL IF I WAS MOVING
SLOWLY OR IF LIFE WAS GOING FAST.
I'M JUST GREATFUL IT'S OVER NOW
AND THAT FEELING DIDN'T LAST

STOP TALKING TO YOURSELF, IT'S WEIRD

need to keep a connection to a reality. any one.
getting sad about things that might not be really is not cool.
it's NOT cool. and you are cool. someone told you that once,
remember? or was that a movie... i think it was both. but it
doesn't really matter does it. did you feel cool? I know you
have done. so that's the one, that's the reality to connect to.
the 'feeling' reality. the reality of feeling. see? you just need
to focus on the positives and then you can make positive
connections. it's like emotional science or something.
you'll see, just try it. it is weird though that you're actually
the one writing this.

How Very Thoughtful

I've used up all the words I know
To illustrate thoughts I want to show
I wish the healing process wasn't so slow

Then all of a sudden the jaws snap shut!
A sneak attack on the alternate

Introvert
(How would they know)
Extrovert
(You're not fooling anyone)

A special exception to the universal rule
That you and everyone else are a part
Of the creation and destruction of
Everything that could and couldn't be...

We, the connected

Looks like someone's trying too hard

How very Thoughtful (cont.)

Sci-fi is cool
Reality is safe
Nihilism exists
Existentialism can fuck off

I want to philosophise
I want to have philosophies
Is anything rhetorical
If nobody is listening

The ending of the story should satisfy
The traveller deserves their trophy

But what made it this far
Not even a rhyme

Apologetic Disbelief

Bitter-sweet relief of nihilism
Ground zero for spiritual cataclysm
What it must be to be a believer!
God? Allah? Satan? Shiva?

Those names accept blames
For endless holy flames
Bare the responsibility
For providing hopeful infinity

But giving my trust to invisible dust
Is an ability I have not
Loaded religions ain't my thing
They're rarely worth a shot

With belief enlisted
My drafted heart could thrive
Jehovah knows I've witnessed
The power of faith, LIVE

Apologetic Disbelief (cont.)

I'm sorry to all the genuine believers
But I fully reject those divine deceivers

The Gods are not dead
Not humbly passed on
You must once have existed
To one day be gone

it isn't what it isn't

face of broken porcelain
turns the smile into a grimace
flipping scales 'tween heavy bitch
and frighteningly thinnest

muscles tear through lack of care
and strain of working focus
patterns, rhythms, flows affected
way to fazed to notice

misleading mix, 3 bags of tricks
an enticing illusion
baking bricks, no bridges fixed
no healing the contusion

greener grass across the pass
just close enough to grab it
now we're free, the grass and me
sliced that nasty habit

THEM

I wrote it all down as soon as I felt
Inspiration, motivation starting to melt

  What will they say
  How will they take it
  Is this the way
  They hope I don't make it

Who knows what "They" means
Paranoid delusion
"They" laugh at my dreams
Encourage exclusion

  Not relatable. Too personal
  No defence. No arsenal
  To fight back the thought
  That this is worth naught

My feelings may change from day to day
But "They" won't disappear
"They" are here to stay

Crab Sticks

Chance encounter, quick reaction
Defensive move gave up all traction
Running sideways, pulled over ground
Bubbles rising make no sound

Faster, faster water courses
Pulled apart by tiny horses
Armour plated endless trip
Release claws, tighten grip

Broken limb goes on ahead
Below becomes all healing bed
Tiny bubbles break the surface
Rushing fate
Current curses

Settle down to deep repair
Broken limb floats off somewhere

(no title)

microdosing on happiness
now, a moment after this
switch flicked quickly
sleepy soft melody
aimless, Miss
microdosing on happiness

Self Esteemed

a black and white great expectation
a process without feeling
a flattering battering
a like
LIKE
smash
subdue
smoke, ash
no clue
sip sip
fight, lose
total lack of concentration
unwarranted elation
fearless
near miss
blanket of security
a process
a great expectation
with no reasonable explanation

(no title)

make a point, sharp tongue
short breath, collapsed lung

sounds good, isn't fun
meaningless to everyone

loneliness be overcome
invited, as a plus one

shouted loud enough to stun

nobody heard

escape

run

Seasonally Affected

Raindrops patter at my window
Reminding me of things I do not know

Grey skies hover overhead
Whispering weird words I've never said

Icy nights prickling my skin
Calm the burning fires deep within

The Opposite of 'In'

I have just discovered
What is really outside
Turns out these four
Indoor walls
Have lied

Kinda Human

Under key and lock, my sweetness
  A rarely acquired taste
As a broken clock lies timeless
  An empty, retired face

A man of tin succumbed to rust
  Wasted, bitterly hurt
Haggard skin's become the dust
  My history in dirt

(no title)

memories reflect my own reality
when actually
everything was different
for everyone but me

Terrible Thinking Problem

Never will I be that extra special one
The unexpected mail you can't wait to open
Not the guy you tell your friends about
Who you hope is there if you go out
The popular one, desired and wanted
A smoking mystery, dark and haunted
Sexy cool dude that keeps it real
Deep and troubled, with a heart of steel
I will never be that extra special one
I'm a drop in the ocean
Make a difference to none

Terrible Thinking Problem (cont.)

Who is that man with all the tattoos
Clearly got something he's trying to prove
Seeking attention with a striking look
Tired old story from a boring book
"Blah blah" That's him, "Oh, poor me"
He should grow some balls
What a pussy
He'll never be special
That posing phoney
Karma got it right
He deserves to be lonely

Scared to be Happy / Not Meant to be Content

I'm frightened
Of hope and expectation
I don't believe in karma
But do I see balance in devastation

Somewhere, someone
Is feeling intense elation
And my misery feels born
Of its delightful creation

But what if I give rise
To hopeful anticipation
Allow myself to be overcome
With positive sensation

Will someone, somewhere
Have their happiness taken
Will my acquisition of euphoria
Completely destroy them

Scared to be Happy / Not Meant to be Content (cont.)

Would it take away their joyous plenty
Leave them bitter, hurt and empty
Just like I am
When wellbeing deserts me

In my husk of a heart
Cheer really doesn't belong
When I'm feeling good
I am just feeling wrong

I think there will always be
This sneaking, creeping suspicion
That being depressed
Is my natural condition

Suzy's Side

I heard about her when I was younger
She's been around
A friend of mine met her once
A few years after leaving school
He wasn't very happy
As an adult we crossed paths, her and I
Flirting, briefly
But it didn't go anywhere
She isn't really my type

Sue makes you think she can change your life in an instant
To be fair she can, but the result is usually the same
Change can be good
However she has no interest in the happiness of others
She stops hearts, throws dreams out of windows
Drowns hopes, cuts family ties

Suzy's Side (cont.)

Seductive Sue
She'll take anyone
Accept any race, welcome any gender, embrace any age
Sounds progressive
Almost enlightened
But it's an illusion
There is no truth in her promises

Sue is not on your side

I really fucking hate that evil, lying, manipulative bitch

Scientific Fuct

Experimental patent
Worth nothing at all
A weak chemical agent
Alone – incapable

Heart frozen in stasis
Cold and still no beating
Reanimation hopeless
Broken central heating

Tested periodically
All truth is proven wrong
Searching idiotically
For substance – there is none

Changing up the formula
Examining components
Technically lonelier
Divided by exponents

Self Pretty

I've written poems about her
And poems about him
Poems feeling great
And poems feeling grim

A poem here, a poem there
Some I keep, some I share
I write about love, and love that I've lost
Once wrote of vengeance and it's terrible cost

I've written poems for fun
And for therapy
But I've never had a poem
Written for me

It's Really Not A Problem

I'm so proud of everything that I write
I roll around in fits of delight
After reading any words I've scribbled on paper
But as the enthusiasm starts to waver
I'm filled with a sense of regret
I suddenly wish to forget
Whatever drivel it is that I have written
Then I'm left with this dark room to sit in
Surrounded by the fear that, at some stage
I will have to write something else on the page
Something much better than I did last time

Or all responsibility I could dismiss!
Just kill myself and be done with this!

I think that would be fine

Be Yourself(ish)

I'd like to be specific
I'd like to be prolific
Can you explain why being me
Sometimes feels horrific

I want to be an artist
I want to be the fastest
Can you help me win the race
No matter what my chance is

I'm a faulty trigger
I'm a failed enigma
Can you please remove my hat
In case my head gets bigger

I killed today
Tomorrow I will slay
Crushing execution
In every single way

I feel my anxiety
So I'll exit quietly
Time to end this nonsense
As I know you're getting tired of me

Spare Any Change

I 'm a writer
I have written
Weak fighter
Don't fit in
Great driver
Not driven
Good hider
Stay hidden
An insider
On a mission
Caged tiger
Never bitten
Getting lighter
No nutrition
Empty chambers
Low ammunition
Lost the magic
A poor magician
Begging strangers
For recognition

My Hero

My vocabulary
Doesn't vary
Enough to make a rhyme
That could stand the test of time

That could one day be
Remembered fondly
Long after I have departed
When the future has started

Although I'm not worried
Legends can't be hurried

A Fucking Poem

To write a poem that is long
Is to write a poem that is wrong
This one's short, in all its glory
If you want something longer
Read a story

An Undeniable Achievement

A worthless treasure
The shortest poem ever

Learning Difficulties

Pen to paper, not that it matters
The secret words between the lines ready
To dissolve into the minds of the readers

Thick, sticky ink left to dry
Left to delight the ignorant
To make the gifted cry

Gifted? Ignorant?
Show me the difference
Tell me a lie

Teach me
Learned reader
As I gouge out my eye

Technical Ability

This poem isn't long
And its content is weak
The rhythm is strong
But not very unique
Or should I say original?
No, that doesn't rhyme

A Deep Analysis of the Creative Process and a Discussion on Artistic Expression, Audience Reaction and Self Criticism

It takes like, an hour
For me to write a poem
That's it

Perhaps that's why
They are all
A little bit shit

Reasons

I used to write

I used to write about my feelings
I used to write about my experiences
I used to write about my doubts and insecurities
I used to write about a life I wished could happen

And how one day all efforts would be rewarded
And how one day all dreams would be fulfilled

And that all judgements would be overlooked
And that all violence would be pacified

I used to write about everything I cared for
I used to write about everything I was
I used to write about everything

I used to write a lot

But then I stopped

Tah-Dah

Well wouldn't writing be wonderful
If words would wrap willingly
Round one another once in a while

Intertwining at attention
Avoiding onomatopation
Obeying their noble overlaying

And not just end out sounding
Like a load of stupid crap

OVERANALYSIS

IT SEEMS TO ME
THE INTENSITY
OF POETRY IS LOST

WHEN WORDS ARE
SMASHED TOGETHER
BUT NO LINES ARE
BEING CROSSED

CHUGGING DOWN A FORMULA
DESIGNED TO MAKE ONE SICK

NO STABBING, SLASHING
AT THE NORMS
JUST A LAZY PRICK

ARTIFICIAL FEELINGS
KEEP THE HUMOUR
HELD IN STASIS

FUCK
SHOULD THESE
WORDS BE HERE OR
SHOULD THEY BE IN
DIFFERENT PLACES

Shared

LET THE PAGES FILL
WITH WORDS PUT TOGETHER
IN A MANNER OH SO CLEVER
READ NEVER
A LOST ENDEAVOUR
SWALLOWED LIKE A PILL

Genuine Appreciation for Growing Support

Smashed it!
Fuck you!
I win!
You lose!
Yo, King! Fight me!
Your loss: likely
Beat me? Your dream!
For me, girls scream!
Me best!
You not!
Head stroke
Blood clot!
I'm great, aren't I?
Handsome
Nice guy
Fuck you!
Sly readers
Please like me!
I need this

Absolutely Mental Health

A follow
They like me!
Oh wait, they do not

A follow
They love me!
No wait, it's a bot

Fuck, I've been unfollowed
My joy has been sorrowed
That dopamine hit
Ended out feeling shit

Hold on a sec
I'll swipe down the screen
Maybe there's likes
Going unseen

Absolutely Mental Health (cont.)

Damn, nothing yet
I'll give it a while
Ahhh one more refresh
Wait. Is this denial?

Surely I missed something
Lost in the feed
Please show me that red dot
I desperately need

Dependent Observer

Fucking online bullshit life
Connection trouble, link chain strife
Bitches tripping over toxic males
Goose sipping cunts treat views like sales
Incelation heats up cringe
Big-ass crotch empowers the minge
Hand-me-down fashion from Ma and Pa
Music's so lame now. D'you think, or nah?

iGroup segregation prevents natural relationships
Too many individuals to unify and end this
Kids/Teens/Youths/Adults
Every person these days
They're just as fucked as ever
But in even dumber ways
Trigger that damn sub atom
With a smiley on your FaceTime
Left or right or Super Like
Swipe swipe, not gonna waste mine

Dependent Observer (cont.)

Stalkers follow invites
Training on their favourite platform
Voyeurs only watching fans
Edging t'wards a transform
Antiquated values
Fuelling cyber-modern thinking
Punk aesthetic pop-goth
Streaming binges, pre-game drinking
Cool is cool, it's all right there
In that offensive thumbnail
'Viral ideas for norms and queers'
Red pills don't make you feel well

flex_bf

Ouch
 That really stung
  when you hung
   me out to dry

Hah
 Feel scathed
  by my words. Bathed
   in the light of your lie

Umm...
 Sorry about that.
  Sometimes I act
   impulsively when I've been drinking

Err
 So how 'bout we meet
  somewhere discreet?
   No no, I know what you're thinking

New World Orders

Show people understanding
And they'll heed the words you say
Show them rage and anger
And they'll want to go away
No one's keen to be told
Of what they should and shouldn't do
Call them stupid, evil, fools
Would that work on you?

Has your mind been changed
By someone yelling in your face
Or are you drawn to souls
Who let you grow at your own pace
Empathy, compassion
And an open mind is crucial
Why be mean and arrogant
When kindness is more useful

Show people that you love them
And the world in which they live
They might just want to listen
To advice you have to give
Now you know, you stupid fool
So go and damn well do it
If no one grasps it first time, please
Stay calm and help them through it

Threatening Pacifism

If someone with booted feet
Kicked your child in the face
Right in front of your own
Would you calmly sit them down
And explain compassionately
How what they did was wrong
And that violence is unnecessary?

It is very easy to cry for peace
When your children are not
Being kicked in the face

Look, Don't

Such injustice plagues this world
All those blood red flags unfurled
Devastation 'cross the sea
Western heads lie comfortably

Tiny ghosts of children made
By giant monsters getting paid
I shall write an angry poem
Yeah
That'll really show 'em

Right This Minute

Knowledge is limited
Voices inhibited
Violence exhibited
Murdering little kids

Help is not on the way
Despite what the guilty say
Innocent people pay
For want of a better way

Make a decision now
Show everybody how
Complacency, take a bow
Excuses not allowed

A View From The Top

Looking out the window
There's nothing left to see
Blinded by a shadow
The light cannot compete

Flames that tell the future
Smoke confirms a past
Flags protect the shooter
Ensuring faith won't last

Sadness shrinks the human
Creatures grow in force
Guided by a few men
Misplacing their support

Looking out the window
There's nothing left to see
But empty shells of sorrow
And bodies of the free

Going Out Tonight

Witness the connected
Highlighted rejected
Trending infected, that viral dead kid

Socials showing hopeful viewing totals
Spilling loud images into the fray
But a million mouths have nothing to say

Real life is a blunt knife
Cuts deep with no point
Watch your temper

Teeth in each other's necks
Taking offence with our mouths full
We all suck

Spit truth. Choke on lies
Carcasses covered in flies;
Every creature on this earth dies

The beauty in error can't be matched by the terror
Of a radical idea. Jammed down one's throat
By the best: The GOAT

Going Out Tonight (cont.)

We're going out tonight to forget the plight
Of those disconnected
To celebrate the resurrected

We're going out tonight
And cutting the slack

We're going out tonight
And not coming back

We're going out tonight
To defend
To attack

observation

silk words slip delicately
half filled glass cracks
white lies through grey teeth
incorrectly placed mirrors
look right, faded pictures
generations carefully disorganised
stories, games, vanity, sleep
dirt, sentiment, blue sky, blue sky
blinds, curtains, dimmer-switch
dark

Poets Anonymous

Fear so strong you could bottle it

Depression with a twist

Brains on the rocks

INSOMNIAHHH

Past has passed
        Future won't arrive
        Now has gone

Bye
        A second guess again
        Night watches me ticking
        To sleep, perchance to scream
        Ay, there's pornhub

Arise!
        Surreal. Weapon unsheathed
        Fighting the natural lighting

Weak. Dazed. Mourning
        Good times

The Feeling

Don't forget to...
Don't forget the...
Remember, everything is...

Memories escape me
I have no idea why
I used to, until lately
But having reached this point

I've forgotten to...
I've forgotten the...
No, it's all gone

I think I thought this would happen
Before long

**This Poem Does Not Have
an Appropriate Title**

Everyone has...

Nobody told me...

One day it will all...

My attention span is definitely getting
Shortbread is quite nice

ONE

PAGE

FULL

OF

TEXT

EACH

WORD

WAITING

FOR

THE

NEXT

LUV U

Roses are white
Violets are flowers
This poem's shite
And it took me hours

I Bet You've Got A Lovely... Oh

I try not to smile
No matter how happy
As my teeth are all broken
And look really crappy

If, at the dentist
I'd tried listening
My teeth would be bright white
And glistening

Instead these brown pegs
That protrude from my mouth
Remind me how quickly
Oral hygiene goes south

Subtext

A poem for no reason
Autumn is a season
Toast is good with cheeson

(no title)

NOT COOL ENOUGH
FOR COOL
NOT GEEK ENOUGH
FOR GEEK
HOW UNFULFILLING
IT IS TO BE
UNIQUE

Words Don't Add Up

Tried to write a poem
Wanted it to rhyme
It's not like I don't know 'em
Writing's hard sometimes
Prompted by ideas
But nothing very real
Encouraged inner fears
To none I will appeal
If nobody is reading
Then should I really care
Planning feels impeding
Éscrire et laissez-faire
Rhymes are overrated
That's why all these are crap
Sorry if you've waited
Now there's no going back
I'll round this up well cleverly
You won't believe your eyes
Sixty's less than seventy
And ten is just two fives

9ku

(9ish haiku)

Myku

I'm a reserved guy
An introvert, you might say
Please leave me alone

Lieku

i don't follow rules
not even for poetry
you can't control me

Pi-ku

I REALLY LOVE PI
THREE POINT ONE FOUR ONE FIVE NINE
SEE, HOW GOOD IS THAT

Terrify-ku

Rah! Boo! Ha! Scared you
You didn't see THAT coming
Oh, you did? Damn it

Die-ku

Boo! It's Halloween
We safely enjoy the scares
Morally bereft

While others fear night
Briefly illuminated
By impending death

Tryku

I don't use big words
If I were clever I would
But I'm not clever

I do try to be
Like, I've read some books and shit
But it doesn't help

One day I will learn
And my poetry will be
Unbelievable

iKu

This is serious
My identity is gone
Someone please help me

Hikeu

I regret coming
My feet hurt and I'm freezing
I want to go home

{quasiKU}

```
-----------
-------
---
-
```

ExPeRiMeNtAl
WORDS language SCRIPT ¿understand?
L a s t F i v e S y l l a b l e S

My First Two Poems

Colours

White is the moon and stars glistening in the night
Or a ghost rising from the dead
The clouds floating through the sky
A piece of paper ready to write on

Red is a tulip from Amsterdam
A juicy red apple ready to eat
My chair I am sitting on right now
Or the red harvest moon in the sky

Green is the grass in my garden
Or the sea with its green sea weed
The colour of my pencil
That I used to write this poem

By Harry Ward, aged 9
(30th September 1995)

ARDNEGASHEL

I sit on the rocks by myself, only me
and watch the jellyfish swim in the sea
It is peaceful and silent
not stormy and violent
A world of salty water
without murder and slaughter
The sea encourages me
to sail in a boat
And just float, float
away

By Harry Ward, aged 10
(1996)

Bonus Poem

This last poem is based on the concept of the early 20th century poem "*Lines on the Antiquity of Microbes*", (or "*Fleas*" as it is also known) by the American poet Strickland Gillilan. The idea was to write the shortest poem possible while still making grammatical sense, conjuring emotion and telling a vague story that could be interpreted by the reader.
I am quite proud of it as it checks all the boxes for being a functional poem, and it also rhymes.
I hope you enjoy it.

A Shocking Discovery

Oh no!

No more poems

(*The End*)

Milton Keynes UK
Ingram Content Group UK Ltd.
UKHW022306290324
440087UK00011B/100

9 781399 980784